New York C[...]

# Broken Open

For Chris,

& for the inspiration & understanding found along the lyrical lines of melodious poetry.

Other works by Garrett Buhl Robinson

<u>Poetry</u>
Martha
flowing stone
Möbius Sphere

<u>Novel</u>
Nunatak

<u>Novella</u>
Zoë

<u>Musical</u>
Letters to Zoey

www.robinsong.nyc

# Broken Open

poems

Garrett Buhl Robinson

ISBN # 978-1511851596

Book and Cover Design
Garrett Buhl Robinson

Cover Photo
Garrett Buhl Robinson

"Intimate with the Ancients" originally published in
*City Fig*, July 23, 2014

"Atom Slice Precise" originally published as a video
poem on YouTube, August 2013

"Emperor Norton's Test of Will" originally composed
in a different version and under a different title for
Ranger Bob

Many of the poems in the collection originally
appeared online on the author's blog and webpage.

Acknowledgement
Epigraph from the poem "In the Public Garden"
by Marianne Moore
from *The Poems of Marianne Moore*, edited by Grace
Schulman, published by Viking Penguin 2003

www.robinsong.nyc

# Table of Contents

## Frost as Fractal Path

## Extending from Within

## Walking Out of the Wilderness

## A Sketch of Breath

## Reflections on the Bay

## Completing a Piece

And what is freedom for?
For self-discipline

— **Marianne Moore**

They tried to trap and kill the bird
to steal the beauty of the song
but gained absolutely nothing.

The beauty is in the singing.
The beauty is in the singing.

# The Way You Say

## Singing for a Living

Music can be taken as a cadence,
a rhythm through which a group may keep stride
and of all the infinite directions,
maintain a singular way together.

Some may say music is a clarion,
a flourish of the flashy, brassy winds
to perk everyone's scattered attention
so they may take careful note together.

Some say music speaks as a familiar,
a soothing voice, an encouraging ally,
a caressing lull that for a moment,
lets one slip away and gently escape.

To me, music is my earnest work
as I chant until my heart bursts:
"The only song that sings for me
is the song I sing by living."

## Street Performer

One peculiar sight I have seen is
a guy who sits all day on the curb
at the world's busiest corner.
As the city folk rush to avoid each other
the urgent surge will often converge
at a crosswalk halt with aggravated faces.

As the crowd stands captivated by the light,
he entices them with a country smile
and opens a divertimento piece
with the little lyric he recites.
Extending this gentle gift he sings,
the melody in the song he breathes,
he charms the crowd till the changing light
releases the winged poems into flight.

## Flowers are Obscene

The kernel's shell is stubborn and tough,
and for good reason.
It fends off the enameled tooth of time
as life deliciously sleeps inside.

Concentrate to the tender tips
of your fingers and pick your seed.
Pour your attention upon it
and witness how the sprout awakens.

Upon the outstretching limbs rise
within the radiance of your mind
and bloom profusions of fruition
in the abundance of your life.

In the denseness, the roots take hold.
In the openness, the leaves unfold.

## Literature and Life

At a local bookstore in your neighborhood,
nestled in the comforts of your familiar town
an author was visiting to sign the book
*Literature and Life* for a thoughtful crowd.

The night moved courteously as it should
but unexpectedly an uproar was aroused
as the people demanded with riling gripes,
"We see the phrases on the pages bound,
and the table of contents' proper nouns,
we see the literature, but where is the life?"

The author said, "These words are dead until they're
    read.
You, the audience, are the life.  May these
words awaken the wings of your mind
and lift your thoughts into heavenly skies."

## What the Simplest Actions Say

Every single moment of every day
we make a statement of our natural state
and the varied ways we socially relate
that through our actions we communicate
and despite whatever we may claim
our interest are with what we are engaged.

Even while we casually walk
every step we take as we make our way
is a definitive declaration
of the immediacy of our place,
the tempo and cadence of our pace
and the direction of our determination.

## Infinite Answer

Pausing for a moment,
the simple man watches
others trample a field
as they play rankling
games of elimination,
then resumes his furrowing journey
turning the earth
while life rises behind him,
opening in flowers
disrobing their petals
swelling into fruit
sweetly encasing sleeping seeds
dreaming into being, while thinking
"The answer is everyone."

## For the Last Romantic

There are some who believe poems are writ
from the themes and theories we invent
as if inspiration was the conscript
of a very specific determinant
that was made with formulas and instruments
so that the unexpected was from intent
and surprise was merely mismanagement
from a factory of ambiguousness.

Then reading your verse earlier today,
listening to the words and all they say,
I began to float on the music they made
from the melodies in every phrase
along the correspondence you arranged
with the chords inlaid and delicately played
and carried by a cadence sustained
by the beat of your heart upon the page.

Poems are not contrived from designs,
they are released from within, deep inside,
and the deeper one's concentration dives
the higher one's inspiration flies,
making brazen leaps to span the divides
in the endless potential of our lives
from the wonder of a child's awakening mind
to the timeless kindness in a grandmother's eyes.

# Medicine in Music

## Poetential

The Bard made the famous statement
about life and the stage but I
wonder for a moment about
the parts each one of us play.

If they are parts, what of the whole?
And in what intricacies
do all these parts turn the endless
mesh of circuits in their roles?

With what diversity may we
cast the communities
and how can these goad or slow
the revolutions of the globe?

Then despite the strict direction
of various acts, scenes and roles,
true beauty is to set
the familiar in the unknown.

## Silly Little Song

The song always gives the bird away
and why he sings is a mystery.
The fact that he continues to sing
is absolutely astonishing.

His only audience is predators.

He carries the shot from the hunters'
guns, he wears the scars from the snapping
jaws, his flesh is punctured by plunging
claws and slithering snakes twist and hiss
around his limbs.  His feathers have been
plucked and his tender toes have been gnarled
yet, he sings as if to awaken the world.

As he climbs higher into the sky,
his song is the wind on which he flies.

## Everyone a Sun

To understand is to dine divinely
and devour without consuming.
The digestion is perception,
dissolving into the dissolving,
the more thoroughly infused,
the more completely ingested.

The sustenance is representation,
spiced with varieties of imperfections,
cascading into the metabolism
of the processes of thought.

No animal is stalked and slayed,
no fruit is plucked, no fields reaped.
Propagate thought through the opening of poetry
and thrive within the enlivening mind.

## Poetry Not Politics

The only direction this poem defines
is toward one's own limitless potential
that extends in every direction
through more dimension than can be imagined.
Strum the universe's strings so reality
hums with resonant music, harmonics
of boggling correspondence with melodic
sequences that resound throughout eternity.

Condemn the poet as vulgar populist,
yet she is more a pragmatic pluralist.
Others may offer their own hard cracked seeds,
and there is no denying the life in these,
yet she offers the progeny of her seeds too
with cornucopias of flowers and fruit.

## Sometimes I Feel

Sometimes I feel I have ground my life down
where I am buried in a mound of dust.

The smooth blocks of time and place I intended
to sculpt into exquisite shapes crumble
into a void and vacant space.

Even the boards I lathe to frame a simple
shelter become snagged with bent nails
that I claw and rail with my shameful pain.

Most of my toil is a miserable mess.

Not every work is a masterpiece, but
the masterpieces may only arise
from the work.  Rare is the time the dust will trace
and the emptiness will clear a way
where a novel idea suddenly appears.

## Be Yourself: Even When You're Confused

Without question, there is a necessity
to reflect, occasionally, upon the past.
Every moment is completely unique
but the particulars are always common.
By considering past predicaments
we may improve our current decisions.

Yet I often find myself falling back
into the cave of a previous place
to find a maze of horror show mirrors
waving with warped distortions
as I seek answers for current perplexities
by speculating on my past uncertainties.

Then comes acceptance – the infinite instant –
only today may answer for today.

## Pleasure in Purity

Not the butterfly
but the fluttering

wafts curling in whirls
of flower fragrance

flowing over steps
of petals nimbly

beckoning opening
nectarous cups

for antennae tippling
and sweet siphoning

through rippling, ringing
endless beginnings

sustaining the winged
leaps of ecstasy

blooming butterflies
becoming the beds

where flowers make love.

# Ambassadors to the Unknown

## Intimate with the Ancients

Through a solitary stretch sketched
upon a parchment surface,

hatched from the brooding memories
of isolations and interactions,

meticulously formulated
into ponderously balanced phrases

carried about clasped to the breast,
surviving rebuke and neglect,

announced from resounding mountains
and sipped with tender attention

through intimate statements
and broadening relations

while retaining rapturous meaning
through transcriptions and translations —

through the extending lengths of space and time
the reach of poets have touched my life.

## Mountain Monument

She struggles up the slick, sloping slights
to make her way where others do not dare.
At times, she pauses in the icy air,
straining and dangling over plunging cliffs
dissolving into soft, beguiling clouds
from stone ledges her aching fingers hold
while watching others casually float,
rising lightly in hot air balloons,
in whimsical, titular ascents,
in precious weaves of other's baskets
adorned with snarky, darling laughter
aimlessly drifting in the wind.

She does not reach for a dizzying height.
She is making a mountain of her life.

## Offhand

Receiving the fellowship's rejection
I have concluded that they must expect
that a disvalued poet past forty
is already set on a trajectory
of inevitable oblivion.
Yet through my long years of dedication
I have sustained a passionate propulsion
of perpetual acceleration
that surpasses escape velocity
as I plunge into the immensity.

Through the unknown I go without delay
as every important discovery
is always made in the infinite space
the parochial shun as obscurity.

## Hazel Hall

Many times I walked by her house.
The second floor in which she may
have stayed over a decade straight
was shroud in trees she'd never seen.
As bare as her view may have been,
no more than gauzed glimpses outside
and taps on the glass to the birds in the sky,
she spun wonders purely of mind
in a chair she could never leave
until she softly slipped to sleep
after whorling skeins into arabesque dreams
now dancing through Portland in her poetry.

## Differentiation

There is a comfort in the familiar.
There is efficiency in the regular.
There is an ease as we lightly trapeze
between the associations which we
are accustomed.  Often we over
look the complexity of our
actions, the underlining mechanics
of our intricately kinetic existence
and follow a formula's arcing trace
through which we are sustained,
stating no more than the easy phrase,
perceiving what is already explained.

I go where no one else goes.
I want to be known by the unknown.

## Nothing

Nothing would lift him up high.
He relied upon his mind.
There were no slopes to climb,
or peaks to aspire
with plunging cliffs at their side,
so he sat and enlivened
his attention on the lines
of interests from the shining
stars that lifted his sight
and the depths of bodies
transformed through time.
The tower on which he rose
was built from the books he composed.

## The Gift of Misgivings

Every accomplishment
is another opportunity
to challenge myself
with a more difficult task,
or so I say in the way
I can prate platitudes.

Yet, I know this to be true –
I may only reach forward
to venture each new step
while the other foot is set
firmly where I previously
stood.

   The opening
opportunities I find are not
from riding upon the shiny
eagle's imperial wings
rising through the sky.
This thought alone is absurd.

The most astonishing steps
are into the unexpected,
and it should be no surprise
that I always find my greatest
breakthroughs when the floor
collapses beneath me.

# Frost as Fractal Path

## Frost as Rhythmic Vision

I had strolled an endless fence line for miles
not knowing what property it defined
or the herd of stock it may enfold.
It was not the stonewall one may expect
but a simple fitting of roughhewn rails
hatchet stripped at the tips to fit in notched
slots hollowed from the old trees' bulging knots.
I followed the trail, amused with the pace
and how my skipping steps did and did not
correspond with the staggering line of posts,
till I lost all sense of time and distance,
enchanted with mine and another's measure.
Then startled to stop by an open gate
with a width for no more than one to pass,
I traced the line winding and climbing
the hill to a cabin set at the edge
of a thick stand of woods covering a slope
that vanished in the roiling clouds above.
A man was sitting on the open porch
and I watched him gently set down his pen,
push the glasses to his glaring eyes, stand
and look curiously down onto me.

## Frost as Interstellar Navigator

As we grow increasingly encapsulated
inside our technologies, integrating
them into our physiology so that
the organs that allow us to process
our interactions with our environment,
the applications of our interests,
the necessities of our developments,
become the ingenuity of our inventions
extending from the corridors which we
construct and where we reside, as they
increasingly stem and bristle throughout our lives.
We will not upload ourselves into our machines,
but rather through time, our machines
will continue to replace our forms and functions,
like minerals slowly petrifying old logs.

Consider this upon the basis of the poetry
of Robert Frost.  There have always been camps
contending his antiquity, his ossified forms
that could no longer adapt with open
plasticity to address the diversity
of contemporary classifications
in the taxonomy of our fascinations.

Yet the charming essence of his perspective,
a touch in the delicate way of a phrase,
is the evocation of the mystery

of an inexhaustible honesty.

We need the astonishment in seeing
how the leaf turns in the breeze, twisting
upon the tenacity of the gentle stem
linking into an ever enlarging involvement
as we follow these delicate threads
lyrically rendering the country colloquial
deepening into the roots holding firm
in the grounds of our existence.

So is the same with our fascination
with the twinkling stars sparkling
in an impossible distance, which can only
be spanned with the abundance of ingenious
imagination.

Yet in the ages to come,
approaching those stars, floating directly
before the magnitude of their emblazoned faces,
contemplating the dynamic complexities
in the fluidity of their currents of convection
and the arcs of their magnetic spectrums,
they will become the affectionate mysteries,
elusively immediate, branching into the open,
and those tiny leaves of life will recede
into the immensity of an impossible distance.

## Frost as Inspiration

At times I climb the harrowing heights
and faintly hear where Frost has set
some of his songs.  No hand can touch that ledge,
those poems rose with a feather's flight
on the steady flow of a lifelong breath
to sing forever in the mountain sky.
I do not expect to reach them.  If I
approach too close, they tighten to silence
and withdraw into another divide.
The only way to reach those rising ridges
is to listen and climb through keen attention.
How can the past be surpassed?  To try
is itself diminishing.  I open
into the all-encompassing unknown.

# Extending from Within

## Renoir

Through his youthful years
Renoir painted dishes,
a lattice of repetition
framing other's meals
he could not stomach
as the blazing kiln
encased each in enamel
in a monotonous shop.

A woman saved him.
Women kept saving him,
leading him deeper
through the beauty
he painted.  He parted
the clouds of the canvas,
reaching to touch
their radiance.

## The Abused Balletomane

Even while he is savagely beaten
and each arising idea of his mind
viciously ripped from him, and his being
torn to shreds while the tattering lines
of his life are hacked and slashed from the dark
by rapacious claws of cowardly monsters
who spoil the world with calumnious remarks
and only aspire to be imposters,
even when he is given poison for drink
and for bread, he is given a stone,
he sternly stands at oblivion's brink
and says, "I will live on beauty alone."
The beautiful movement gracing the stage
is all he needs for his life to be sustained.

## Under the Ocean

Instead of depressed, I am the bottom
of a vast basin with the whole ocean
dropped on top of me.  There are no waves
alternating, there is only the weight
of the crushing darkness of the deep.  Even
here I will sing and when I open
my lips for the music's release, the sea
floods into me and the tiny beads
of bubbles seep in a lightening string
slowly floating up through the soundless leagues.
In each, a delicate song I have squeezed,
tiny spheres the entire weight of the sea
cannot defeat, till they bulge and breach
and rise with the moon's full majesty.

## Touching Up the Endless Finish

In the morning, after the sweet refreshment
of a soft night's sleep and the ritual of a morning
    routine,
the professional dressed in her solid suit
follows the lines of the morning paper
as her spry mind is enlivened with the prospects
of the market's day while riding the subway.

In the evening, drained, having given all
the energy she had reserved for the day,
returning home, she simply sits in her seat,
listening to the droning sound of travel,
plunging through the deep tunnels
as the heavy cars clack along the rails.

The distinction is blurred between the carrier
and the carried, as the whole world moves together.

## On First Looking into John Rawls'
### *A Theory of Justice*

Reading John Rawls is like watching Spinoza
work. The propositional statements opening
every paragraph distinctly outline a frame.
Then the ensuing declarations reveal the delicate
curve of the lens. One would expect a coarseness
in the grind of gritty words, a gnashing of gears
in the machinery of technicalities, but the dust
clears with the soft breath of insightful inspiration
revealing a clarity in vision, not simply of the text,
but of the world.
                I imagine Keats' "First Looking,"
climbing steep slopes of verdant folios from within
Baruch's humble chamber, diligently polishing
the mind into a never-ending understanding
resolving the focus of everyone's spectacular life.

# Rockaway

Stretching my hand into the giving mist
dissolving and obscuring as the tips
of my fingers touch the unyielding rock,

I trace the features with the lines I climb,
forming phrases over the solid shapes,
lifting my weight upon the jagged crags.

My rope waves beneath me, swaying freely
in the void until I no longer know
how high I've climbed, as I have never known

how far I must go, not to reach a height,
but to cover a length of time
that is defined as long as I am alive.

## For Marianne Moore

Ms. Moore, I have read your work from place to
place, hunkering over the pages to savor
the way your nimble feet tip toe across
the page with every step as light as it is sure.
The poems are a guiding line of lanterns
extending through passages of detailed grandeur
where the protean shapes that you portray
are a lively menagerie, not exhibiting
human qualities, but revealing virtues
essentially and effortlessly natural.
And now for the first time in my life
I am reading your poetry in Brooklyn
finding the greatest paradox you ever penned
is your numerous versions of perfection.

# Walking Out of the Wilderness

## For an Actor

On stage, as through her life, she stands
with grace and beauty at either side.
Truth shines before her.  Accomplishment
towers behind her.  She embodies
calm confidence in the dignity
of her endless beginnings.
She draws the audience into her world
as she pours herself out before them.

At first, they hear what she says.
Then they see what she is saying.
Then they feel the performance hall
fill with the emotion of her expression
as their senses are inundated
in the lapping waves of the engulfed
theater.  Then, so softly they barely
notice, the audience floats from their seats.

## Place in Nature

She too was once an egg receiving the rupturing
seed.  She too rested within an instinctively
woven nest, encased in a speckled shell.
When she awoke and broke into the open,
she was pushed and nudged toward the edge.
When she felt the freshened breeze of nurturing
wings arriving to feed, she was shunt aside
by beloved cuckoos and coddled dandies.

But now, the breeze beneath her soaring heights
dispels the twaddling, squawking duress.
It is true, she was shoved from her nest
but she fell into flight and now she fills the sky.
This nobody dismissed as nothing
is the phoenix endlessly rising.

## Making Musical Metaphors

The key of the fitting piece is engagement,
the tuning of attention upon the minutiae
from where the immensity unfolds.
There is a rhythm in reading, following
the lines deeper into the composing mind
stretched across a tenuous distance
and displayed in radiant arrays of all
that is suggested.  There is always the flux,
the slipping space between what is said
and what is read, and through this movement
pour yourself into the ever deepening mystery
to trill your thoughts with your experience
until the sonorous lines arise
so you may make music of your life.

## Moon of the Mind

They rejected the day for the light of the moon.
The moon falls behind, but eventually overcomes,
as each lagging path catches up again.
Then renewed, the moon may eclipse the sun.

Although it wanes, it also waxes, and gently
shines in the sky, offering illumination for guidance,
without a searing glare.  And even though the sun
rises to begin each day, it abandons us every evening.

Then our eyes must adjust and we are sent stumbling
upon the abysmal pits of darkness.

From this they say they would rather embrace the
    night
and the capricious course of the lunar light.

Yet the sun does not set.  What we know of day
is an unwavering star.  Night is our own shadow.

## Instrumental

Some say he fell flat,
others that he shrilled sharp,
but one way or another
he chased the other

players away.
They can complain
that he is out of tune,
but I prefer to say

he was simply
ascending and descending
a different scale,

an emptiness
and an impetus
to create new arrangements.

## Reflections upon Rembrandt's
### *Anatomy Lesson*

Through my whimsically wandering thoughts
treading through the unruly wilderness
of countless past experiences
there is an image I find myself
frequently encountering – Rembrandt's
*Anatomy Lesson.* The instructor
stretches the sinews with the forceps,
the muscles of his own forearm straining,
as if pulling Apollo's bow for the flight of light
while the other hand waves with luminous phrases.
Amazement flickers on the crowd of students' faces
as they pour their attention into the open body,
into the mystery of our existence,
the being we are, the enigma we live.

## The Living Arts

The task is daunting — to assemble sundry
eccentric pieces into a seamless whole,
a composite of ephemeral whims,
fanciful delights populated with spectral
images outstretched upon the tossing seas
of dreamy sleep.  Each piece is essential.
Then to lift this up onto the stage
and caressed with curtains, warmed with lights
and released to roam through the endless fields
of the audience's converging minds,
bring this lyrical creation to life.
Listen to the sweet release in sighs of delight
as the touch of each tender phrase swells our
solitary bubbles till they pop with astonishment.

## Atom Slice Precise

Envision this,
a keenness of resolution
in perception
atom slice precise.
Instead of observing a solid object,
see all the composing atoms
bound in molecules and bouncing,
not in erratic movement,
but in intricately interactive rhythms.

Envision the shapes of sound
rippling through space
flooding an auditorium,
filling the vast chamber
with pulsating waves
lapping upon the encompassing shore
of every drumming ear in the audience.

Envision the motion of stars
wheeling in clusters
spinning around a center of gravity
immeasurably singular,
a dancing fulcrum
upon which massive
celestial bodies revolve.

Then consider the world we see
and envision what it may be a reflection of.

# A Sketch of Breath

## Living Mystery

There is a fog between us.
There is a fog throughout us.
It is so subtle we seldom notice
until we reach for what we are
convinced we see and nothing
but ribbons of mist
seep between our fingers.
We never realize how blurred
our vision is until we try tracing
the fine lines between us,
lines that a touch will
break and fray and send
us abjectly falling away.
The lines are strings of attention
drawn with our breath
through the mist of existence.

## Poetry

There are rooms on pages endlessly
extending to where defining lines
converge to meet at infinity.
They unroll and unfold at teatime
with polite dolls sailing on fleets of toys
over seas of intricate invention
animated in the unexpected ways
of a child's innocent openness.

In these harping and hopscotch games
that are played with a musical phrase
and image conveyed, we may escape
the numbing routines we accept as fate
and rediscover the child that finds
the universe awakening in the mind.

## Nothing Plain

In my desolate directions
there is no end to loneliness.

I bewail my bewilderment
into the expressionless emptiness
filled with numbing silence.

I have reached to others
but my blundering ways
only cause others dismay.

I speak, but there is nothing
plain in what I say.

So I sit at my desk with a pen
to formulate the shape of a phrase
that I carve into the bald
marble of the page.

## Push by Producing

I express my opinion
in the manner of my living.
There are others who disagree,
but there will almost always be
others who disagree about
practically everything and now
I am simply waiting for them
to disagree with disagreement
and then, for a pristine instant,
a perfectly, heavenly moment,
we may all be contently appeased
before the next eruption of nattering.
Then, I resume my protesting
by diligently not speaking.

## Mark Question

In regards to labels I draw a blank.
Just as most anyone else, I have been
called what others misthought of me
as well as what others had hoped would hurt,
but in countless times when I've made mistakes
what I've called myself has been the worst.
However, if you insist I will say
with the most confidence I can enlist
having realized that my destination
is every moment in which I exist
that all conclusions are inconclusive
and the only absolute I can give
is
  if you feel you must label me
  then label me a mystery.

## Reflections on John Keats' fragment:
### "This living hand"

I recall, as so many others would,
the sad, fragmented song's withering lines
that I had recited numerous times.
If we had only read and understood
those lines practically written in Keats' blood
as he lie in bed waiting a touch of ice
while beautiful Italy shined outside
in a quaint village on a rocky slope.
The lapis lazuli sea does not coax
as he gasped for breath while he bled inside
hemorrhaging where no one else could see.
The mind may sing, but the body is broke.
I think of verse, this mild, frivolous art,
and how many die of a broken heart.

## Product and Process

Open a book and step inside
another person's fascinating mind.

Recently, I have been reading Rawls'
careful distillation of a lifetime of
scholarly thought.  His work is a vast
palace where passages lead through
balancing chambers of impeccable
order openly arching for illumination.

Of course, my preference is poetry.
Verse sets my mind in the motion of music,
an ecstatic dance partnering with the
discovery of a new interest appearing
through the focus of attention gazing
into another's eyes – the enrapture
of my greatest love – the beautiful beyond.

Literature is not information.  Information
is simply the incarnation of what
we feel to be thought.  It is the platform
for the engagement — the process.
It is no more the life of the mind
than the floor is the dance.

Open a book and step inside
another person's fascinating mind.

# Reflections on the Bay

## True Love

The everlasting lady of creation
stands in a flowing robe with a naked sword
turning into a plow with its tip to the ground.
Her other hand raises a stem of grain
to express with assurance – "Abundance"
at the entrance to the Golden Gate Park.
The statue was dedicated to mark
John Muir meeting President Roosevelt.
Through the thick foggy mist of early morning
while sauntering through the fronds and flowers
I noticed someone had spray painted the word
"Love" on the statue in the dark night before.
Information may be in what is said,
but meaning is made in the way we say it.

## Emperor Norton's Test of Will

Being Emperor Norton
   was never an easy task,
every one of his reigning days
   were challenged with countless tests.

Once, while he passed a tavern
   overflowing with merriment,
the crowd begged him to enter
   for his jovial accompaniment.

They pulled a chair from the table,
   a throne at the table's head,
and everyone crowded around
   to hear whatever he said.

They filled a tall mug with beer
   and set it before their friend,
and eagerly awaited
   to hear what stories he'd wend.

Then with an obnoxious jostle,
   a stranger shoved through the crowd,
and stood before the Emperor,
   a sour and envious lout.

Then as the crowd grew silent
    the stranger shrilly complained,
"I know they call you Emperor,
    in whatever foolish game,

but I must claim the contrary,
    despite what all I have heard.
To call Falstaff emperor
    is absolutely absurd."

The Supreme Emperor Norton,
    turned toward the stranger's face,
to see if the hateful remarks
    were simply made in play.

The stranger could not resist
    to add more disparaging brays,
dismissing anyone's doubts
    whether the ass had more to say.

"And who do you think you are
    swilling quaffs of beer,
as if you haven't a care
    whether you can walk out of here?

Who would appoint you Emperor
　　upon which you stake your fame,
upon what powers do you rule,
　　on what grounds do you make your claim?"

The Emperor paused politely
　　to hear this stranger's say
and let him vent his fury
　　of what had angered him today.

Then he gently parted his mustache
　　and calmly stroked his beard,
then slowly lifted his mug
　　to sip a tipple of beer.

He took a warm breadth deeply,
　　and released a soothing sigh,
then decided he would answer
　　before the stranger picked a fight.

"There is no question of my position
　　and that I rule over the land,
because every single person
　　faithfully obeys my command."

Perhaps the response was too clear,
    or perhaps he thought it curt,
because the stranger recoiled
    as if the gentle phrase had hurt.

His fists clenched beside him
    and his face grew red as a beet,
the stranger began to holler
    while furiously stamping his feet:

"How can you say such a thing?
    How can you make such a claim?
Others may call you Emperor,
    but I say you are insane.

There are teams of kings and Presidents,
    Ministers and Judges alike,
that have tried to lead the people
    and keep them in the right.

Yet still they all have failed,
    and people strayed every time.
No leader has had the strength
    to keep everyone in line."

Then the Emperor shook his head
    in disbelief with his guest,
then let out a bellowing laugh
    that bounced his tasseled epaulets.

Then after a suspenseful pause
    so the commotion was hushed,
the Emperor began to explain
    to clear the confusion up.

"Friend, your anger is in vain,
    your fury is for yourself,
and with my magnanimity
    I will offer you some help.

It is true that I have made the claim
    to be Emperor out and out,
and that everyone obeys my command,
    there cannot be a doubt.

Friend, let your heart by merry,
    come and drink your fill,
the command I made for everyone
    is that they do just as they will."

# Completing a Piece

## Just a Poet

I am just a poet.
I just make musical suggestions.
I may shape beautiful worlds with outstretching
gardens that are indistinguishable from the
surrounding forests
and mountains encircle the settlements with steep
slopes garlanded with fresh water flowing directly
from the heavens
and the towers in the towns reach directly to the stars
as if the tip of each pinnacle touches Polaris
and the sky pivots and revolves on this point as much
as the world spins from the cynosure
and all the town is composed of palaces
accommodating everyone's life and mind and
expanding endlessly with everyone's interest
and there are lively markets of the exotic and
common alike where everyone can afford to pay
top price so that the merchants are as pleased as
the customers
and everyone dances
and everyone sings
and every single thing is fascinating,
but they are fantastic,
they are abstract,
and I am just a poet.

## Explaining Experience

As this pen dances in my hand, a line
unspools a thread of music in its loops
that I carefully tighten until they're tuned
as they stretch through the distance between our
    lives.
Although these strings may tie, they do not bind
as they are played in the ways we move
in progressions of corresponding chords
and syncopations of delightful surprise.
Whether it is the sweetness of a voice,
phrases woven into a tapestry,
the color of touch, the taste of a choice
or the music and rhythm in imagery,
to pour emotion into poetic form
is a synesthesia of our sensory.

## Inspiration (A Sketch of Breath)

More than a breath — a simple breeze
that could be relatively anything
diffusing into emptiness —

a song
that turns into every attentive ear
allured with the sweet ease of melodies
composed to please from the birds of verse
that these fluttering pages release.
Feel the tickling, urging
with the delicate sweep of wings
humming as the airy song fills
the brightening sky of your mind.
Say yes to the music.
Say yes by listening.

## The Way I Play

Ever wonder how ideas develop?
They often accumulate through the long
solitary stretches arising from
within the mind's engaged contemplations
revolving ponderous thoughts considerate
yet isolated while settled and seated
in quiet confines.  For me, it is a
manner of life till I touch the sharpened
tip with a fountain and feel the cleansing
flow of poetry playfully tumbling
down the steep ravines that lyrically sing
with rivulets of beautiful music
choiring with the confluence
that wash me into the open ocean's deep.

## Book Stand

With a modest little stand,
and my humble little books,
I sit outside every day
reading poetry to the passing
masses, and amidst the roar
of the colossal machine
that is New York City
I softly and sweetly sing.

People have kicked over
my stand and scattered my books,
and I gather them up again,
re-arrange them in display,
settle back in my seat
while I continue to sing.

## Completing a Piece
— for Robert (Kobi) and Kate Kobayashi

Beginning with a lump of clay
and then running on the pedals
the potter turns the potter's wheel.

There is a wonder in standing
and watching the artist's imagination
take shape in the palpable world
and transform the plain into the beautiful.

With a few last touches that swirl
as the standing vase spins, the wheel
slows and the piece becomes fixed
where it is fired inside the kiln.

Then after a caressing of paint
it is softly set on display
to suggest all it may contain.

## Broken Open

I have seen a whole tree
grow through a crack in stone
and through the winter cleave
the rock to make a home.

In the spring the broad limbs
sing with the perches they provide
then summer with the fledglings
that fly into the sky.

Then the autumn turns
into the cooling days
and leaves as the sunlight burns
in a falling, glorious blaze.

The seasons change,
yet I remain.

## Yes Keats

— In Memory of Professor Edwin Murdoch (Ted) Stirling

At my stand in the freezing degrees,
reading the public poetry while they
shuffled by in their bulging winter bundles,
I sat smiling.

Briskly passing, one lady made a point
that she is an author too and had bought my book
and read it, then pausing, she turned
on the marble steps

and said, "You are an excellent writer."
before running inside and out of the cold.
Her kind phrase kept me warm
the entire day.

Behind me, I could hear the ice cracking
in the frozen fountain hardening into
a solid, cloudy pool with a few flakes
of flurried snow

drifting in swirls upon the surface
at the bottom of an ornate basin
of stone overseen by a statue of a sage
lifting his head

in tireless preparation to make a meditative
declaration distilled from a lifetime
of careful contemplation.  The statement is
never stated.

A fitting figure for a frozen world.
Yes Keats, the wisdom is kept and left unsaid,
never disclosed or exposed to a world's
denigrations,

retained in the perfection of detached
consideration.  Let us chisel your name,
again and again, in the frozen flow
of ageless stone.

# Notes

Pg. 15   This poem opens with a reference to Shakespeare's lines, "All the world's a stage and all the men and women merely players." *As You Like It*, Act II, Scene VII

Pg. 38   Inspired by Robert Frost's statement, "My utmost ambition is to lodge a few poems where they will be hard to get rid of."

Photo by Ray Baltazar